The Color of KENOSHA

A Coloring Book for All-Ages
from Kenosha, Wisconsin

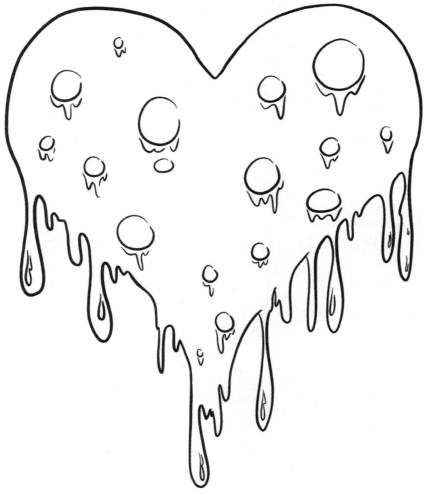

Created by
Donovan Scherer

The Color of Kenosha:
A Coloring Book for All-Ages from Kenosha, Wisconsin

Text & Illustrations Copyright © 2020 by Donovan Scherer

Published in 2020 by Studio Moonfall LLC

All rights reserved.

This is a work of fiction. Names, characters, places, and incidents are products of the author's imagination or are used fictitiously. Any resemblance to actual events, locales, organizations, or persons, living or dead, is entirely coincidental.

No part of this book may be used or reproduced in any manner whatsoever without written permission, except in the case of brief quotations embodied in critical articles or reviews.

For information regarding permission, write to:

Studio Moonfall LLC
5031 7th Ave
Kenosha, WI 53140

ISBN: 978-1-942811-16-9

www.StudioMoonfall.com

Bring out the crayons!

The idea for this book unofficially began back in March 2020. Pretty sure that was 700 years ago by now.

When it was clear that this summer was going to be a bit different than my usual running around to comic conventions and local markets, it was time to adapt. While I've been making printable coloring pages for a while, mostly through my Creature of the Week series, there were people out there that needed something to do while locked in their houses and dang it, I could do something about that.

With my day job and show schedule wiped out and the new Studio Moonfall shop (come see it at 5031 7th Ave!) temporarily shut down after being open for only a little while, it was time for a weird idea. Or maybe A Coloring Book of Weird Ideas.

That book started with random ideas from people's suggestions drawn into whatever fun nonsense my imagination would twist them into. Every day there would be a new idea and every day it would go out into the world for anyone to print it up for free to color. And if they wanted to throw in some extra support, there'd be a book on the way.

Between starting on March 15th and at the time of writing this on July 27th, I've put out 175 free coloring pages of weird ideas, zombie beans, fantasy monsters, and more. And now, illustrations for my neighboring businesses.

Knowing how much Studio Moonfall was struggling with the world we were in no longer being familiar, I figured I wasn't the only one having trouble. And if people out there were enjoying these little critters I was drawing up, maybe I could help bring that same sort of fun to other small businesses.

So, here are some of your favorite local businesses and attractions run through the filter of your local indie author/illustrator and bookshop owner, Donovan Scherer.

Happy coloring!

SPECIAL THANKS TO ALL THE BUSINESSES INVOLVED IN MAKING THIS BOOK

Apis Hotel & Restaurant
Author D. Lieber
Backyard Dream Studios
Blue House Books
Boathouse Pub & Eatery
Captain Mike's
Copy Center
Dooley & Associates
EXP Realty
Gateway Service Center
Harbor Park Crossfit
Heal Therapies
Jake's Kenosha Area Weather Page
Jay's Recovery Resource Center
Jerry Smith Farm
La Fogata
Leting's Landscape, Lawn & Snow
Lou Perrine's Gas & Grocery
Marina Garden
Mike Bjorn's Clothing
Paddy O's Pub
Public Brewing Co.
Sazzy B's
Slick Vic's Barbershop
Steampunk General Store
Studio Moonfall (that's me)
Tawwater Sign Co.
TG's Restaurant & Pub
The Buzz
The Garage
Union Park Tavern
U.S. Taewondo Academy
Waterfront Warehouse
&
Visit Kenosha - Kenosha Area Convention And Visitor's Bureau

LEARN MORE ABOUT THEM AT:
www.ColorOfKenosha.com

U.S. Taekwondo Academy

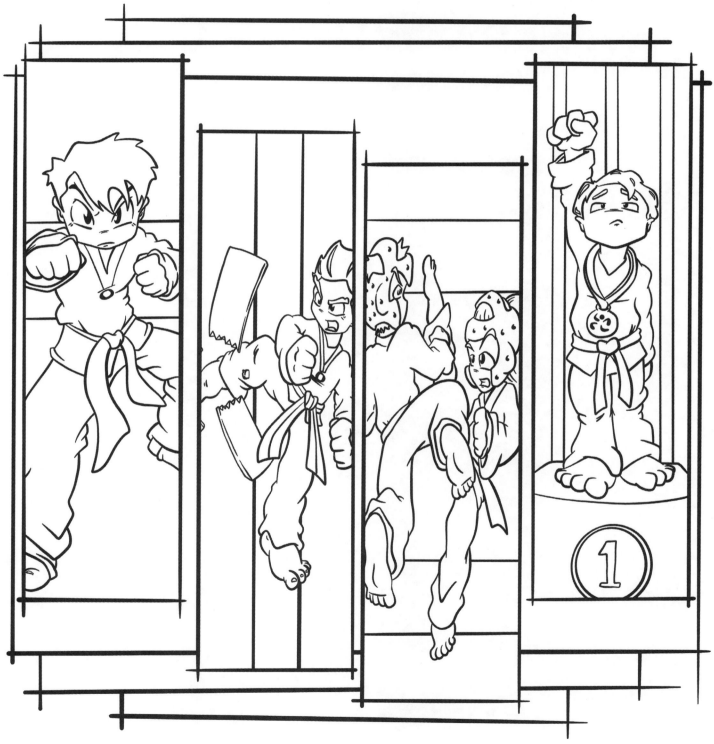

WANT MORE TO COLOR?

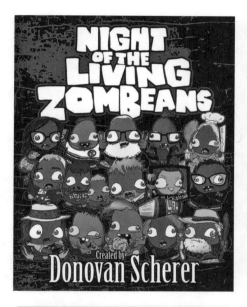
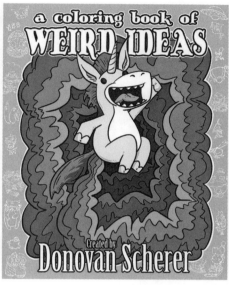

SIGN UP FOR MONTHLY COLORING BOOKS AT:
WWW.PATREON.COM/DONOVANSCHERER

For more all-ages adventures in horror, fantasy, and science fiction by Donovan Scherer, the creator of this book, please visit:

www.StudioMoonfall.com